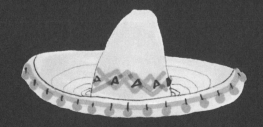

Cats in Hats

Cats in Hats

Illustrated by **Jo Clark**

Text by Jonny Leighton

First published in Great Britain in 2020 by LOM ART, an imprint of
Michael O'Mara Books Limited
9 Lion Yard
Tremadoc Road
London SW4 7NQ

A CIP catalogue record for this book is
available from the British Library.

Papers used by Michael O'Mara Books Limited are natural,
recyclable products made from wood grown in sustainable
forests. The manufacturing processes conform to the
environmental regulations of the country of origin.

ISBN: 978-1-912785-29-2 in hardback print format
ISBN: 978-1-912785-33-9 in ebook format

1 2 3 4 5 6 7 8 9 10

Designed by Ana Bjezancevic
Printed and bound in China

www.mombooks.com

*Disclaimer: No cats (or hats) were injured
in the making of this book.

ENTER THE CAT FLAP

Do you like cats? Do you like cats in hats? Do you like cats in wigs, cats with fruit on their heads or cats that look a bit like celebrities in an adorable but slightly disconcerting way?

Yes? Congratulations, you have a niche interest and are in the right place.

No? What are you doing here?

If you're sticking around, why not push your head through the doors of the moggiest milliners you'll ever come across and find out what awaits you on the other side …

INTERGALACTICAT

A long time ago, in a cattery far, far,
away, there was a cosmos-striding,
evil-empire-destroying, sci-fi
super-cat, ready to kick some
butt and save the universe.

Or is she a moggy with two
cinnamon buns stuck to her head?
The truth is we'll never know.

CLAUDETTE

This French fancy is a beret-wearing cat. She enjoys brie and the occasional Gauloises on a crisp, spring day. She starred in the Palme Paw winning New Wave film alongside Meowliette Binoche.

What do you mean she's some sort of cliché? Ferme ta bouche!

AMEOWLIA EARHART

Some cats take to the skies to hunt down their feathery playthings and some do so in the spirit of exploration.

Ameowlia has heard of a desert island full of palm trees that make the perfect scratching posts. The only problem is that it's way out in the Pacific, where neither cat, dog nor man has ventured before.

Godspeed brave kitty, Godspeed …

BARNABY FLUFF

Pull up an oar and take a relaxing
trip down the river with this furball
of a boat cat. Enjoy a glass of wine
and watch the world drift by.

There's just one rule: NO SPLASHING!
If you splash, you'll go overboard.
And it'll take an awfully long time
to wring the river water out of
your boater, so be warned.

HOT BUNS

The Easter Bunny has a lot on, what
with making and delivering chocolate eggs
to boys and girls, as well as adults who
have a hole inside them that can only be
filled by overpriced, novelty chocolates.

Even cats have to do their bit and Hot
Buns is happy to help – for a price.
She accepts cash, card or catnip.

'CALL ME FISHMAEL'

That Captain has a lot to answer
for, dragging Fishmael out across
the ocean on a fool's errand.

He doesn't even really like fish,
let alone big, white whales. He's
more of a bird cat, himself.

Look at the poor guy. He's seen things
out there on those waves. I know
someone who deserves a belly rub ...

THE
WIDOWMAKER

Who doesn't love a cat that wears hats in
the form of the birds she kills and drags
in through the cat flap at three o'clock
in the morning? Tell me, who?

The Widowmaker is one stone-cold
kitty. Up trees, on the roof, no bird
is safe from her vicious pounce.

(She's also looking for a
home. Any takers?)

MISS AMY

They tried to make this cat go to rehab,
and luckily … she did. Quite frankly,
the catnip situation was getting out
of control – everyone could see it.

She's doing really well now,
thanks for asking.

STETSON SALLY

This snowy cowgirl knows the difference
between a 'moo' and 'meow' and now
she's off to round up some cattle. There's
nothing like galloping across an open plain
on an Appaloosa, with the wind in her fur.

What? You've never seen a cat
ride a horse? You haven't lived.

SAD SIMON

A fez is the perfect hat to hide big secrets. Like how Simon isn't really as aloof and cool as he makes out. Sure, he might lift his tail in the air and walk past you with a look of disdain that could put someone in hospital, but really ...

... he just wants to be petted.

MR SCORCH

This friendly neighbourhood kitty would
like nothing more than to help you put
that fire out, but the whole 'cats don't like
water' thing is really getting in the way.

Let's just all agree that he looks
like hot stuff in his jaunty hat.

PURRMIT THE CAT FROG

Cats love to be dressed up by their owners – the sillier the outfit the better. A knitted frog hat, for instance, will fill your cat with joy. (Ignore the scratching as you try to put it on its head.)

Purrmit is currently having a bit of an identity crisis. Is she a frog or a cat? Who knows? Either way she is one cute kitty.

TUTTI FRUTTI

'There's something on my
head, isn't there?'

MC COOL CAT

This cat is not just wearing a hat, she IS the hat. There's almost certainly a life lesson here for all of us, if you just look hard enough.

MC Cool Cat brings the party. Are you dancing? Yes, I'm asking.

EXISTENTIAL FRED

From time to time we all have an existential crisis. For Fred, his hit him like a freight train when he was licking his bum for the 345th time that day.

Is this the kind of cat I want to be? What life am I on, the sixth? Time's running out, Fred … time's running out …

BLONDIE

It's a terrible misconception that
blondes are dumb, naive and artificial.
Although, in the case of this cat, I'm
afraid all of it is completely true.

Blondie has an ongoing feud with the
other cat that lives with her. Funnily
enough, though, it only appears
when Blondie looks in the mirror.

TRICKY DICKEY

Talk about cunning. Tricky Dickey
is taking his mousing duties to the
next level, going behind enemy
lines in this dastardly disguise.

Those mice will be completely
fooled by this hat. How could
they possibly see past it?

DAVID MEOW-IE

This Aladdin Sane tribute cat took it all too far but boy could he play guitar.

(No mean feat given he doesn't have opposable thumbs or any formal training.)

NURSE KITTY

What more could you need than this
nurse to get you back to health?
Sure, he can't give you an injection,
but who needs medicine when
you're with a cat this cute?

Warning: cuteness is no substitute
for professional medical help. This
cat accepts no liability for any
illnesses, real or imaginary, from
which you may be suffering.

BECKY WITH THE BIG HAIR

What? You've never seen a cat with a candy-floss-coloured giant afro before? You haven't lived!

Becky is happy to share her style advice, just so long as you throw her a couple of compliments first. Or, maybe, a treat.

PURR-PLE RAIN

Look into the eyes of this
cat. He knows exactly what it
sounds like when doves cry.

(Mostly because the doves couldn't
understand why a cat in a pouffy wig
was chasing them round the park
singing Prince songs VERY badly.)

BATH CAP KITTY

'You told me we were going upstairs
to snuggle. Why am I wearing this hat?
Step away from the tub, Susan, I did not
agree to this. You'll never take me alive.
Not the bath – anything but the bath!'

EL CATO

Sometimes a cat just has to get
the sun out of his eyes, and look
incredibly cool at the same time, *si*?

El Cato is partial to a margarita with
a nice wedge of lime and a salted
rim. So, when you're ready...

PEONY PUSS

This avid gardener waited a little too
long to be let back into the house
and now some of the flowers are
slightly lacking in, erm, petals. Oops.

Those weren't your prize roses, were
they? Good. Because she ate them, too.

DR FUZZ

When times are tough,
cats just want to help, too.

Dr Fuzz is the finest medic known to
cats. Just don't expect her to waste
time on bedside manner. She's here to
cure you not charm you, goddammit!

Now someone pass the scalpel.

McFURBALL

What exactly is it about this cat that makes you think it's Scottish? The tartan hat? The ginger fur? For the last time: he can't play the bagpipes!

However, McFurball's band, Scotch Whiskers and the Highlanders, are actually available for private functions, so do just ask if you'd like an entertaining four-piece for weddings, birthdays and highland jigs.

QUEEN OF
THE CATS

They might have built the pyramids but
those ancient Egyptians have a lot to
answer for. Cats have never got over
the superiority complex of being treated
like royalty. This one even has a tiara.

So-called 'owners' are mere servants to
most cats. And don't you ever forget it.

PAWS 2: THE SQUEAK-WEL

Dun dun... Dun dun...

Just when you thought that it was safe
to go back in the water, a creature from
your worst nightmare emerges: PAWS!

Actually, Paws only gets mad when
you steal his spot on the couch.
So, if you lose a leg, don't say
you haven't been warned.

SIR HATSALOT

Most cats own us, rather than us owning them. This upper class cat is just a bit more obvious about it.

Sir Hatsalot doesn't care if that offends you. Sir Hatsalot owns you.

AVOCATO

They say that if Millennials really want to buy a property, all they have to do is save the money from the constant avocado brunches they're always gorging themselves on. Don't they have ANY self-control?

Well, if Big Avocado is going to give away a cat with every one of its delicious fruits then I couldn't care less about getting on the property ladder. Show me the Avocato!

CHEF NIBBLES

'Table for two in the corner?'

For the fussy cat in your life, why not arrange for a purr-sonal chef to cater to all their whims? Chef Nibbles here rustles up a distinctive *duck à l'orange*.

But just so you know, the *l'orange* part of the dish may or may not be related to the furballs Nibbles is prone to coughing up. Don't say you weren't warned.

THE CATUE
OF LIBERTY

Behold! Beacon of democracy, keeper
of the burning flame of liberty that
burns inside the breast of every woman,
man and child who values freedom –
the Catue of Liberty. Follow her light
and she'll never steer you wrong.

(I mean, she'll try not to. That's actually
a lot of pressure to put on one cat.)

CLEOCATRA

Did you know that Cleopatra was actually a Greek? Or that she probably had red hair? And that she probably wasn't as beautiful as we make her out to be? And that she was actually in Rome at the time of Julius Caesar's assassination?

Or ... that she was a cat?

BIG BEN

What do you get if you cross
a cat with a clock? Ticks!

And for this terrible joke, this
cat will be hailing a cab, heading
straight to the airport and flying
away, never to be seen again.

FANG FATALE

We all know that cats are terrified of snakes, or anything that looks vaguely similar, like a cucumber. Honestly, look it up on YouTube. Hours of fun.

This kitty's hair is literally made of snakes. That's why she's looking you right in the eye – there's no way she's looking up!

NEOPAWLITAN

Wanna pizza this pie? It comes with
all the toppings you could ask for:
cheese, tomato, olive and ... cat.
Delivery is free and guaranteed to
arrive on time and piping hot.

Wait? Cat? Did someone say 'cat'?

RUSTY THE MAIL CAT

Rusty has places to be and mail to deliver and NO he will not beware of the dog. He isn't afraid of no hairy human-loving mutt with attachment issues and he also doesn't have a problem with chucking parcels over the fence because, guess what? He's not your personal butler, he's just the mail cat.

OK?

TERRY THE TRUCKER

Terry has a family in each service station across the land and he lays his head in a new bed every night. It's not a life for everyone but some cats just suit being on the road.

Check out his great cap. If that doesn't make #trucklife worth it, what does?

Honk, honk!

HAPPY
HOLLY-DAY

Holly has been a very good cat this year
and for Christmas she would like:

1. To follow you around 24/7 for no
particular reason. (But also disappear
for worryingly long stretches of
time when she feels like it.)

2. To sleep directly on your chest
making it incredibly difficult to breathe.

3. To use your curtains as scratching
posts even though you bought her
a deluxe scratch perch last year.

THE SNOWCAT

Follow the Snowcat and she'll take you
on a magical adventure through the skies
and up to the North Pole, where she will
introduce you to all her snowcat pals.

In the morning, you will wonder if
it was all a dream. I am here to tell
you that it was. You need to seek
urgent medical assistance. You have
had a hallucinatory episode.

SYDNEY THE CULTURE CAT

One is elegant, sophisticated, emblematic of a certain kind of modernity, almost unquestionably an international icon and a stylish symbol of progress and culture that will endure through the ages.

The other is the Sydney Opera House in the form of a hat. On a cat. Let that sink in.

STEADY TEDDY

Sometimes being a kitten is not enough – you have to go one step further to make sure people know you're the cutest one in town.

That's why Teddy here is dressed up as a bear. There's no doubt who's getting all the cuddles.

NOËLLE THE CHRISTMAS CAT

It's Christmas time, which means just one thing: Noëlle gets to play on the Christmas tree again. Last year she smashed fifteen baubles and left the Christmas lights strewn across the carpet from the lounge to the kitchen.

She never quite made it to the star at the top, though. But she's got a feeling that this will be her year. It's her one Christmas wish.

THANKFUL KITTY

Pumpkin here would like to thank all the
mice for being so much fun to chase, the
birds for being entertaining to watch,
the dog's bed for being so comfortable
and herself for being so fabulous.

THOR

With his pointy helmet, control over lightning and thunder and super-feline strength, Thor might look fearsome …

… but really he just wants cuddles. Like every cute cat out there.

Bye.

About the illustrator

Jo Clark graduated from the Cambridge School of Art in 2010 with a master's degree in Children's Book Illustration. She has since launched a successful range of greeting cards, gift, homeware and stationery with her popular illustration style. She has always loved animals and wants her work to promote kindness to all species, as well as make you giggle. As a vegan, she is always looking for new technologies to reduce the environmental impact of her products.

 joclarkdesign.co.uk   Joclarkdesign   @Joclarkdesign